D1602799

Queen Elizabeth

and England's Golden Age

Chaucer
Celebrated Poet and Author

Dante
Poet, Author, and Proud Florentine

Eleanor of Aquitaine
Heroine of the Middle Ages

Galileo
Renaissance Scientist and Astronomer

Machiavelli
Renaissance Political Analyst and Author

The Medicis
A Ruling Dynasty

Michelangelo
Painter, Sculptor, and Architect

Thomas More and His Struggles of Conscience

Queen Elizabeth and England's Golden Age

Leonardo da Vinci
Artist, Inventor, and Renaissance Man

MAKERS OF THE MIDDLE AGES AND RENAISSANCE

Queen Elizabeth

and England's Golden Age

Samuel Willard Crompton

CHELSEA HOUSE
PUBLISHERS
A Haights Cross Communications Company ®
Philadelphia

COVER: Queen Elizabeth I in coronation robes c. 1559.

CHELSEA HOUSE PUBLISHERS
VP, NEW PRODUCT DEVELOPMENT Sally Cheney
DIRECTOR OF PRODUCTION Kim Shinners
CREATIVE MANAGER Takeshi Takahashi
MANUFACTURING MANAGER Diann Grasse

Staff for Queen Elizabeth
EXECUTIVE EDITOR Lee Marcott
EDITORIAL ASSISTANT Carla Greenberg
PRODUCTION EDITOR Bonnie Cohen
COVER AND INTERIOR DESIGNER Keith Trego
LAYOUT 21st Century Publishing and Communications, Inc.

© 2006 by Chelsea House Publishers,
a subsidiary of Haights Cross Communications.
All rights reserved. Printed and bound in China.

A Haights Cross Communications ✦ Company ®

www.chelseahouse.com

First Printing

9 8 7 6 5 4 3 2 1

Library of Congress Cataloging-in-Publication Data

Crompton, Samuel Willard.
    Queen Elizabeth and England's golden age/Samuel Willard Crompton,
        p. cm.–(Makers of the Middle Ages and Renaissance)
    Includes bibliographical references and index.
    ISBN 0-7910-8632-1 (hard cover)
  1. Elizabeth I, Queen of England, 1533–1603–Juvenile literature.
  2. Great Britain–History–Elizabeth, 1558–1603–Juvenile literature.
  3. Queens–Great Britain–Biography–Juvenile literature. I. Title
  II. Series.
    DA355.C94 2005
    942.05'5'092–DC22

                                            2005007491

CONTENTS

Young Princess

Princess Elizabeth of England was born on September 7, 1533. Her father was King Henry VIII and her mother was Queen Anne Boleyn. Almost everyone in England knew about King Henry VIII's marital troubles. In 1529, he had started divorce proceedings against his first wife, Queen Catherine. She had given birth to one daughter, but no sons, and King Henry wanted a son to serve as heir to the throne.

The pope, as leader of the Roman Catholic Church, denied King Henry's request for a divorce. Letters flew back and forth between London and Rome, all to no avail. The pope would not change an earlier decision, which had allowed King Henry to marry Queen Catherine in the first place. Queen Catherine was first married to King Henry's older brother, Arthur. After Arthur died, Catherine received special permission from the pope to marry King Henry.

With the pope unwilling to grant him a divorce, King Henry formally broke ties with Rome and the Roman Catholic Church in the spring of 1534. He announced that he and his people were no longer part of the church. They were now members of the new English Catholic Church. King Henry was the head of this new church and he held as much power in it as did the pope.

With this new power, King Henry VIII granted himself a divorce from Queen Catherine. He married Anne Boleyn almost immediately. He had been in love with Anne Boleyn for many years.

King Henry VIII started divorce proceedings in 1529 against Queen Catherine, his first wife, to marry Anne Boleyn. His divorce petition is shown here.

People said she had cast a spell on him, and it seemed that the people were right, for he had done monumental things in order to marry her.

King Henry and Anne Boleyn married in the spring of 1533. Their child, Princess Elizabeth, was born that September into a very dangerous time. Her aggressive and impatient father made many enemies, both through his changes to the church and with his military policies. As long as her mother, Queen Anne Boleyn, was in the people's favor, Elizabeth had nothing to fear. If her mother fell from grace, however, Princess Elizabeth would be in great danger.

As the years went by, Anne Boleyn kept her looks. People remarked on her fine black eyes and great style in dancing, but King Henry seemed less and less interested in his wife. He had done huge and momentous things in order to marry her, but she had failed to provide him with a son.

King Henry believed he must have a son to follow after him, that the country needed a male ruler. He believed that England could not be ruled by a woman. King Henry's father, King Henry VII, was the first of the Tudor family line. The Tudors were not an ancient family. They had come to the English throne in 1485. They could not afford to have the crown pass to a woman. No, King Henry must have a son.

In the spring of 1536, King Henry granted himself a divorce from Anne Boleyn. As leader of the English Catholic Church, he had the power to do so, as he had previously done with Queen Catherine.

Anne Boleyn was charged with adultery and treason. Found guilty on both counts, she was beheaded at the Tower of London in May 1536.

Young Princess Elizabeth now had no mother and her father showed no interest in her. King Henry, meanwhile, was already planning his next wedding, his third. In 1536, King Henry married Anne Seymour, who had been one of the ladies-in-waiting to Anne Boleyn. King Henry was happy for a time and he was extremely happy when Jane Seymour gave birth to a son named Edward. King Henry finally had a son and a male heir.

King Henry's joy was short-lived, however. Queen Jane Seymour died just a week after giving birth to Prince Edward. King Henry mourned her deeply. He seemed to have genuinely cared for her.

Princess Elizabeth found that her servants now called her "Lady Elizabeth." She asked them why, but she was too young to understand that she had been disinherited and was no longer considered a princess. Her father had announced that she was an illegitimate child, as was her older half sister, Princess Mary. Both of them were now mere ladies of the court, princesses no longer.

During his life, King Henry VIII had a total of six wives. They were: Catherine of Aragon, with whom he had a daughter, Princess Mary; Anne Boleyn, with whom he had a daughter, Princess Elizabeth; Jane Seymour, with whom he had a son, Prince Edward; Anne of Cleves, with whom he had no children; Catherine Howard, with whom he had no children; and Catherine Parr, who out-lived her husband, but bore him no children. It was clear that King Henry would eventually have to decide which of his three children would become king or queen.

Growing up among the members of her father's royal court, young Elizabeth came to fear and distrust men. Her father was a dangerous man. He lost his temper often and sometimes struck his servants. Sometimes he even had his counselors beheaded. He had been a good man in his youth, many people said, but he had grown tyrannical and mean as he got older.

Now in his 50s, King Henry lived a risky, fast-paced lifestyle. Not only did he take chances riding and hunting, but he was also a robust eater. Plates of food and goblets of wine disappeared from his

King Henry VIII (shown here) had a total of six wives and three children. Elizabeth, his daughter with Anne Boleyn, would eventually became queen of England.

table. No one was going to risk sending the king into an outburst by telling him he should stop eating so much.

While King Henry ate and drank in excess, young Elizabeth grew in grace and knowledge. She was always a very pretty girl and, by the time she was 12, she was one of the tallest girls among those her age. She also loved her books very much and she learned a great deal, reading in Greek, Latin, French, and Spanish. All of her tutors agreed that she was a very intelligent child.

Lady Elizabeth often read and studied with her older half sister, Mary, and her younger half brother, Edward. The two princesses and the prince got along well in these early years. All of their mothers were dead and their ferocious father was unapproachable, so they relied on each other. Then, in January 1547, came the news. King Henry was dead.

Test Your Knowledge

1 When was Princess Elizabeth born?

   a. 1533

   b. 1544

   c. 1535

   d. 1543

2 What did King Henry VIII do with his new power?

   a. Passed new laws

   b. Granted divorces to his people

   c. Granted himself a divorce

   d. Put on lavish festivals for the people

3 During his life, King Henry had a total of how many wives?

   a. Five

   b. Seven

   c. Four

   d. Six

4 How did young Elizabeth feel about men?

   a. She was not aware of them.

   b. She feared and distrusted them.

   c. She admired and trusted them.

   d. She loved and looked up to them.

5 In what year did King Henry VIII die?
   a. 1547
   b. 1548
   c. 1555
   d. 1565

We Wished for Our Elizabeth

S hortly before he died, King Henry VIII made out his will. He insisted that Parliament, which consisted of the House of Lords and the House of Commons, make his will into English law. King Henry's will removed the taint of illegitimacy from Elizabeth and her half sister Mary. Both were acknowledged

11

as true English princesses, but neither would inherit the throne.

King Henry believed in the rule of men. Even though Prince Edward was the youngest of the children, he would inherit the throne. The king's will went on to say:

- If Prince Edward died without any children, the throne would pass to Princess Mary.

- If Princess Mary died without any children, the throne would pass to Princess Elizabeth.

- If Princess Elizabeth died without any children, the throne would pass to Lady Jane Grey, a second cousin of the three royal children's.

King Henry had always been the type of man that people obeyed. Even from the grave, he would influence future events. As a result of the royal will, Prince Edward became King Edward VI in 1547. Although King Edward was not yet ten years old, he was already very intelligent. No one expected a young boy to know all about the kingdom, however, so he had the advice and counsel of several older

Prince Edward, the youngest child of Henry VIII, inherited the throne when his father died. Prince Edward (shown here) became King Edward VI of England.

men. One of them was Lord Dudley, who became the Duke of Northumberland.

Elizabeth was delighted to be a princess once more, but she knew the royal court was full of dangers. She was closely guarded in what she said. No one really knew what she was thinking.

Elizabeth was on good terms with the new king, her younger half brother. One of her earliest letters, among those that still survive today, was addressed to him: "Indeed, when I call to mind the particular benefits of the most good and most great God, I judge this to be the greatest all: that He has quickly and mercifully restored you to London after your recent illness."[1]

Young King Edward was often ill. "Into which I think indeed that you fell by some special providence of God, just as I wrote in my recent letter to your majesty, so that every occasion of illness has vanished."[2] Elizabeth went on to say, "Nothing is so uncertain or less enduring than the life of man, who truly, by the testimony of Pindar, is nothing else than a dream of shadows."[3]

Young Elizabeth, 13 at the time, knew something about the uncertainty of life. She had seen several

The Marriages and Children of King Henry VIII

First marriage: Henry VIII and Catherine of Aragon (They are divorced in 1533.) Daughter Mary, born in 1516; dies in 1558.

Second marriage: Henry VIII and Anne Boleyn (She is beheaded in 1536.) Daughter Elizabeth, born in 1533; dies in 1603.

Third marriage: Henry VIII and Jane Seymour (She dies soon after childbirth in 1537.) Son Edward, born in 1537; dies in 1553.

Fourth marriage: Henry VIII and Anne of Cleves (Marriage is annulled.)

Fifth marriage: Henry VIII and Catherine Howard (She is beheaded in 1542.)

Sixth marriage: Henry VIII and Catherine Parr (She outlives her husband, who dies in 1547.)

Mary, Elizabeth, and Edward were half brothers and sisters. Lady Jane Grey was a second cousin to all three of them. Mary, Queen of Scots was their first cousin, once removed.

people come and go in her life already. She concluded by saying, "To which providence I commit
the protection of your majesty, and at the same time
ask that he keep you safe and sound for the longest
possible time."[4]

Elizabeth had a special bond with her half
brother King Edward. They were both firm
Protestants. King Henry VIII had separated
England from the Roman Catholic Church, but
he had kept many of the former rituals in his new
English Catholic Church. King Edward VI and his
counselors changed these rituals. By requiring that
every church in the nation use the new Book of
Common Prayer, they ensured that England would
become a truly Protestant country.

While Princess Elizabeth and King Edward VI
were both Protestants, their sister Princess Mary
was Roman Catholic. There was also a generation
gap between the siblings. Mary, born in 1516,
had grown up in an England that knew only
the Catholic religion. Her two younger siblings,
Elizabeth and Edward, born in 1533 and 1537
respectively, had grown up in a country that leaned
toward Protestantism. The gap between the siblings

was mirrored by the gap between the English people themselves. Almost everyone under the age of 20 or 25 tended to be Protestant, while many of those over the age of 40 tended to be Catholic.

King Edward VI died in the spring of 1553. He was only 16, but he had suffered from consumption (an illness now known as tuberculosis) for some time. The boy king was dead, but King Henry VIII's will had been quite explicit about the royal line of succession. Princess Mary would now be the queen of England. Many English Protestants feared, however, that Queen Mary would try to turn them into Catholics once more. A rebellion broke out right away.

The Dudley family, led by the Duke of Northumberland, supported Lady Jane Grey for queen. She was a second cousin to Elizabeth and Mary, and she was a good Protestant. The Dudleys took her to London and had her crowned. Meanwhile, both Princess Mary and Princess Elizabeth escaped northward.

Despite the turmoil, many English people turned out to support Princess Mary. Even those men and women who feared her Catholicism, still believed she was the rightful queen. Many of them were also impressed by the courage she showed in the face of danger. Within two weeks, Princess Mary had raised an army and was marching on London.

As the resistance melted away, Princess Mary entered London in triumph. She was accompanied by Princess Elizabeth, who rode by her side. The two sisters were triumphant. The rebel leaders were sent to the Tower of London and many of them were later executed.

Princess Mary enjoyed a splendid coronation in 1553. She made a good beginning with her new subjects, but she surprised many when she announced that she intended to marry her cousin Philip, the future king of Spain.

Not only was Queen Mary a Catholic, but she also wanted to bring England back to the Catholic faith. Marrying the most powerful Catholic prince in all of Europe was a good way to do this. With Philip by her side, Queen Mary would be able to require all of her subjects to observe the Roman Catholic faith—or so she thought.

Even before Philip arrived, Princess Elizabeth was in trouble with her half sister. Everyone

King Edward VI died in the spring of 1553 of what we believe today to be tuberculosis. As specified in the will of King Henry VIII, Princess Mary took over the throne and became Queen Mary (as shown here).

who knew Princess Elizabeth was sure she was
devoted to the Protestant faith. She was often seen
reading religious books and pamphlets about
Protestantism. However, Queen Mary thought
she could bring her younger sister around. For
months, Queen Mary kept asking when Princess
Elizabeth would worship at the royal chapel with
her. Princess Elizabeth did come, at times, but she
often did not attend services, pleading illness. At
other times, she came to the chapel, but did not
stay for the entire Mass. By the start of 1554,
Queen Mary had become deeply suspicious of her
younger sister.

On March 17, 1554, a group of officers and
soldiers came to take Princess Elizabeth to the
Tower of London. Nothing could provoke as much
fear in young Elizabeth as the tower. This was where
her mother had been executed in 1536. This was
where traitors went to receive the king's or queen's
justice. Princess Elizabeth begged the officers to
allow her to write to Queen Mary. If only the queen
would agree to meet her, Princess Elizabeth felt
sure she could win her over. Apparently Princess
Elizabeth thought she had great influence over

Queen Mary, while Queen Mary thought the same thing of Princess Elizabeth. The letter began:

> If any ever did try this old saying—that a king's word was more than another man's oath—I most humbly beseech your majesty to verify it to me, and to remember your last promise and my last demand: that I be not condemned without answer and due proof.[5]

Only Princess Elizabeth would have used the word *demand* in a letter like this.

"I am by your Council from you commanded to go unto the Tower, a place more wonted for a false traitor than a true subject."[6] Princess Elizabeth knew that many people went into the tower, but few ever came out whole and healthy once more.

> I protest afore God (who shall judge my truth, whatsoever malice shall devise), that I never practiced, counseled, nor consented to anything that might be prejudicial to your person any way or dangerous to the state by any mean.[7]

Princess Elizabeth begged Queen Mary not to believe the stories that were being spread about her. Princess Elizabeth insisted that she was a good and faithful subject. She concluded by saying "Your highnesses' [*sic*] most faithful subject that hath been from the beginning and will be to my end, Elizabeth."[8]

Princess Elizabeth carefully drew long horizontal lines down the length of the rest of the paper. She did not want anyone to insert other words and claim they belonged to her. Handing the paper to the officers, she learned that, during the time she had taken to write the letter, the tide of the Thames River had changed. It was now too late in the day for her to go to the tower. Princess Elizabeth had bought herself another day of freedom.

Queen Mary did not even read Princess Elizabeth's letter. She was already persuaded that her half sister was a traitor. Princess Elizabeth was sent to the Tower of London the next day. What was behind Queen Mary's suspicions? Despite the fact that Princess Elizabeth was a Protestant, she was becoming the favorite among the common people. At age 20, she was many years younger than her half sister and far prettier. Princess Elizabeth had turned into a beautiful young woman and her charm was even greater than her beauty. Queen Mary saw that the people preferred Princess Elizabeth, and this upset her.

Princess Elizabeth, meanwhile, spent two months in the Tower of London. She was treated well when she was there and after two months she was allowed to come back to court. She was not present for the wedding between Queen Mary and King Philip of Spain, however, which took place in the summer of 1554.

Queen Mary desperately wanted a child. She had waited a long time for marriage, but now she was disappointed in her husband. King Philip seemed to have married her for political reasons. He was not warm toward his wife and he often disappeared for months.

The year 1554 was a decent time for Queen Mary, but her life and reign soon began to enter a period of decline. Queen Mary thought she was pregnant in 1555, but this turned out to be a false hope. Meanwhile, King Philip kept his distance from his wife, who seemed to grow sadder and lonelier with each passing day.

Sometime in 1555 or 1556, Queen Mary decided to require the English people to become Roman

Catholics once more. Lacking the help of her husband, Queen Mary tried to do this on her own. She announced that Catholic Mass would be held in all churches throughout the land. She also began persecuting those Protestants who would not renounce their faith.

The people's fears were coming true. This forced conversion to Catholicism was exactly the reason some people had supported the rebellion in favor of Lady Jane Grey, but it was too late now. Mary was queen and she would do as she pleased.

Queen Mary soon turned her unhappiness on others. She ordered that those Protestants who would not renounce their faith be executed. In 1557 and 1558, some 300 leading Protestants were burned at the stake for refusing to renounce their religion. People began calling the queen "Bloody Mary."

While Queen Mary became more and more unpopular, Elizabeth's popularity continued to rise. The common people had always liked her. She reminded them of her long-dead father, King Henry VIII. As the years had passed, people began to forget about King Henry's tyrannical nature. They began instead to remember the handsome man he

Sometime in 1555 or 1556, Queen Mary decided to require the English people to become Roman Catholics once more. She began persecuting those Protestants who would not renounce their faith. The execution of Protestants at Smithfield in 1557 is shown here.

had been in his youth. As they recalled King Henry more favorably, they began to transfer this favor to Princess Elizabeth. A set of poems began to extol the virtues of Princess Elizabeth, while condemning Queen Mary:

When Margaret Eliot, being a maid,
After condemning in prison died;
When lame Lamarock the fire essayed,
And blind Aprice with him was tried;
When these two impotents were put to death,
We wished for our Elizabeth.[9]

Princess Elizabeth would not have to wait long for her time as queen. Queen Mary was ill. While Elizabeth held her own court at Hatfield House, her favorite residence, many courtiers quietly drifted away from Queen Mary's court and came to Hatfield.

Queen Mary weakened during the summer of 1558 and died that November. News of her death spread very quickly. Messengers rode to Hatfield House, where they found Elizabeth sitting under a tree reading in Greek. She had always been a lover of many languages. When they told her that the queen was dead, Elizabeth rose and quoted from the Bible, "This is the Lord's doing, and it is marvelous in our eyes." She had already slipped into the practice of using the royal "we."[10] In November 1558, at the age of 25, Princess Elizabeth became queen of England.

Test Your Knowledge

1 Parliament consisted of the House of Lords and

a. the House of Royals.

b. the House of the People.

c. the House of Commons.

d. the House of the Monarchy.

2 According to the royal will, if Prince Edward died without any children, the throne would pass to

a. Princess Elizabeth.

b. Princess Mary.

c. Princess Grace.

d. Prince Henry.

3 Young King Edward was often

a. ill.

b. angry.

c. traveling.

d. happy.

4 King Edward died from an illness we now know as

a. the plague.

b. scarlet fever.

c. German measles.

d. tuberculosis.

5 How many Protestants were burned at the stake for refusing to renounce their religion?

a. 200

b. 450

c. 300

d. 500

ANSWERS: 1. c; 2. b; 3. a; 4. d; 5. c

makers of the middle ages and renaissance X makers of the middle ages and renaissance X makers of the middle ages and renaissance

The Queen and Her Suitors

Following the death of Queen Mary, Princess Elizabeth became queen immediately. Although the formal coronation did not take place until January 1559, Elizabeth held power from the first moment of the news of Queen Mary's death. Although she was only 25, Queen Elizabeth was wise beyond her years. She

29

had learned a great deal about survival, first in the court of her dangerous father and later in the court of her dangerous half sister. By the time she took the throne, Queen Elizabeth was a master of disguise and concealment.

Even Queen Elizabeth, however, needed a good set of counselors. She turned to William Burghley, a firm Protestant who had attracted her attention some years before. In the same month that Queen Mary died, Queen Elizabeth gave Burghley his written instructions. He would be the leader of her privy council and was not to hold back, even if he thought his wishes differed from hers. She wanted his complete confidence and confidentiality, and she promised the same to him. This was the beginning of a remarkable partnership that would last for the next 40 years.

While William Burghley became the queen's trusted advisor, there was another man whom Queen Elizabeth loved with all her heart. He was Robert Dudley. Born in the same year as the queen, Robert Dudley came from a very ambitious and successful family. His father had become Duke of Northumberland and had been beheaded for leading the rebellion in favor of Lady Jane Grey. Other Dudleys had also come to terrible ends. One of them had been beheaded early in the reign of King Henry VIII. These losses never prevented the Dudleys from being admired, feared, and envied, however.

Robert Dudley was an exceedingly tall and handsome man. One of the best portraits of him shows an elegant man with a narrow beard. His height made him stand out at court, and Queen Elizabeth made him horse-master, which meant he found, bought, trained, and prepared the horses for all court affairs.

In the first year of her reign, Queen Elizabeth made it clear that Robert Dudley was her favorite courtier. She showered favors upon him and flirted shamelessly with him. Rumors began to spread around England that she was pregnant with his child.

If the rumors had proven to be true, they could have caused a tremendous scandal. Although the English people as a whole loved Queen Elizabeth, she had always had some critics, and Robert Dudley was a married man. If Queen Elizabeth were to have a child with a man who was already married, her entire reign would be cast into scandal.

Dudley's wife, Amy Robsart, generally stayed at their country estate, while he spent all of his time in London or wherever Queen Elizabeth took her court. The queen was fond of conducting what were called "royal progresses," moving from one castle to another. The royal progresses meant less expense for the queen because the nobleman in whose house she lodged had to pay for all of the food and beverages. Queen Elizabeth and Robert Dudley may have been the grand couple of the moment, but he was a married man.

While there were many people who wanted Queen Elizabeth's hand in marriage, the only one she loved was Robert Dudley. Then, in the autumn of 1560, disaster struck. Amy Robsart was alone one afternoon. She had sent her servants away, telling them she was fine on her own. When some of them returned, they found her lying dead at the bottom of a staircase. Her neck was broken. Many people suspected that Robert Dudley had arranged to have his wife murdered. Queen Elizabeth could not be associated with such a scandal. Though

Queen Elizabeth had many male advisors and confidants.
Sir Robert Dudley (shown here) was, however, most likely
Queen Elizabeth's one true love.

she loved Robert Dudley deeply, she sent him away from court until the preliminary investigation was complete.

Months passed and the rumors continued. In faraway France, Mary, Queen of Scots is said to have exclaimed, "He has murdered his wife and Elizabeth is going to marry her horse-master!"[11]

Elizabeth and Her Favorites

Robert Dudley was the most favored man in Queen Elizabeth's court, but he was not the highest-ranking member of the court. Elizabeth had a great assembly of high-ranking nobles. The English system of nobility was based upon tradition and length of service. The longer someone had been a knight, a count, or a duke, the more important he was to the queen. The amount of time one's father, grandfather, or great-grandfather had been in that position was also important.

The two greatest lords of England were the Duke of Norfolk and the Duke of Suffolk. As their names suggest, the Duke of Norfolk governed the northern part of the realm, while the Duke of Suffolk ran the southern part. These two men competed with each other to be the leader of the queen's armies.

When the results of the investigation arrived, Amy Robsart's death was found to have been accidental. No charges were levied against Robert Dudley, or anyone else.

Slowly, cautiously, Queen Elizabeth brought Robert Dudley back to court. He continued to receive signs of her favor, but she was never as

Queen Elizabeth did not especially like either man. She was pleased, however, to divide power between them, while grooming men like Robert Dudley to compete, as well. Queen Elizabeth learned this tricky means of power from her father, King Henry VIII, who never let his nobles know where they stood. They were always anxious and seeking the king's or queen's favor.

Some men became great nobles through their service to the queen. Elizabeth raised William Cecil's status and made him an earl. She knighted the common seaman Francis Drake. These actions were shrewd. By rewarding people who were loyal to her, Queen Elizabeth maintained their loyalty. She did make some costly mistakes, however.

outwardly affectionate toward him again. She may have loved him profoundly, but being the queen was most important to her. She worried that her subjects would think less of her if she married a man who had been suspected, however briefly, of murdering his wife.

While Robert Dudley faded out of favor, other suitors made their desires known to Queen Elizabeth. Many foreign kings and princes wanted her hand in marriage. Even King Philip of Spain, previously married to Queen Mary, showed an interest. Through his ambassador, King Philip proposed the same sort of arrangement he once had with Mary. He and Queen Elizabeth would marry, but she would remain the sole sovereign of England. He would be free to come and go as he pleased, especially to watch matters on the continent of Europe. Queen Elizabeth gave several polite "no" answers to King Philip. She did not wish to be married the way her half sister had been.

There were plenty of other offers to consider. The crown prince of Sweden, who later became King Eric IV, courted from afar. So did Archduke Charles of Austria. Henry, the Duke of Anjou, in

France, also courted from a distance. Queen Elizabeth did not take any of these men very seriously. She saw clearly that she was in a winning position. These men wanted her and, as long as they wanted her, they would be friendly to England. If she chose to marry any one of them, the others might gang up on her. She politely accepted their gifts and told them she would think about the matter, and this went on for years.

The English Parliament kept urging Queen Elizabeth to marry. Parliament was second in importance only to the queen. The members of Parliament practically begged her to marry a foreign king, so there would be heirs to the throne. The members feared the same thing that King Henry VIII had feared long ago—that there would be no son, no male heir, to carry on.

Queen Elizabeth answered Parliament in January 1563:

I know now as well as I did before that I am mortal. I know also that I must seek to discharge the great burden that God hath laid upon me; for of them to whom much is committed, much is required. Think not that I, that in other matters have had convenient care of you all, will in this matter touching the safety of myself and you all be careless.[12]

She made no promise to marry. On the other hand, neither did she say that she would never marry. Elizabeth left her options open, so she could respond to the changing circumstances of the times. The ability to react to change was one of her greatest talents.

This particular talent, however, also drove her chief counselors to distraction. William Cecil was beside himself because the queen would never commit to anything. She always wanted to consider all of her options. Soon, however, a matter arose from which she could not back away—the matter of Mary, Queen of Scots.

Test Your Knowledge

1 How old was Princess Elizabeth when she became queen?

   a. 32

   b. 23

   c. 25

   d. 22

2 Queen Elizabeth and William Burghley formed a partnership that would last for how many years?

   a. 40

   b. 30

   c. 50

   d. 15

3 Why did members of Parliament want Queen Elizabeth to marry?

   a. Because the country would be more stable

   b. Because Queen Elizabeth would be happier

   c. So there would be a king

   d. So there would be male heirs to the throne

4 What was one of Queen Elizabeth's greatest talents?

   a. The ability to react to change

   b. Her political knowledge

   c. Her ability to ride horses

   d. The ability to decorate the royal palace

5 What drove William Cecil to distraction?
   a. The queen's beauty
   b. The queen's inability to commit
      to anything
   c. His secret love for the queen
   d. His desire for more power in the
      queen's court

ANSWERS: 1. c; 2. a; 3. d; 4. a; 5. b

First Cousins, Once Removed

Queen Elizabeth, born in England in 1533, was one of King Henry VIII's daughters. Mary, Queen of Scots, born in Scotland in 1543, was the daughter of King James V. The two women were first cousins, once removed. This meant that Elizabeth was a first cousin to King James V. The relationship between

41

Queen Elizabeth and Mary, Queen of Scots would prove to be the most difficult relationship of Queen Elizabeth's life.

Elizabeth became queen of England in 1558. One year later, Mary became queen of France. Mary was only 16 at the time, but she was married to the eldest son of the king of France. When that king died in a jousting match, she became the young queen of France.

People were fond of comparing Queen Elizabeth of England and Queen Mary, who was both queen of France and queen of Scotland. Queen Mary was taller. She was slightly less than six feet tall. Both women had clear, flawless skin. Both were excellent horsewomen, but there the comparisons ended. Their personalities and characters were quite different.

Queen Elizabeth had grown up in a dangerous time and place. She had learned the art of stage presence as a very young girl. Queen Mary had grown up in splendor, as a member of the French royal court. She faced no dangers. Queen Mary excelled at her studies, but she never developed as clever a mind as her cousin.

Queen Elizabeth was a Protestant queen. Queen Mary was a Catholic queen. The differences between the two continued from there. Queen Mary had grown up as a member of the French royal court. She became queen of France in 1559, but she enjoyed that honor for only one year. When her young husband died, Mary became a widow at the age of 19.

In 1561, Queen Mary decided to return to the land of her birth, Scotland. She had been smuggled out of Scotland when she was very young and her whole life had been something of a sacrifice to the old alliance between Scotland and France. Now, she wanted to see the kingdom of her father, and to rule it.

Queen Mary sent letters to her cousin, Queen Elizabeth, asking for passports, so that, if the sea turned dangerous and rough, she might turn into an English port for safety. Queen Elizabeth refused the request, pointing out that Queen Mary had not honored the terms of an earlier agreement between England and Scotland, but Queen Mary set out for Scotland anyway.

Mary, Queen of Scots landed in Scotland in 1561. She had been away since she was five years old.

The Scottish people barely knew her. There was a religious difference between them, too, and it was turning into a wide chasm.

Raised among the members of the French royal court, Queen Mary was an ardent Catholic. When she left Scotland at the age of five, most of her people were still Catholic, but a great change had taken place. Religious reformer John Knox brought the beliefs of John Calvin to Scotland and many, if not most, of Scotland's people were now Presbyterians (the Scottish branch of the Calvinist Church).

Even someone as skillful as Queen Elizabeth would have found this a very difficult situation. Queen Mary, however, lacked her cousin's skill with people and she was not wise enough to admit that fact. Queen Mary had a half brother, an illegitimate son of the previous king, King James. This half brother told Queen Mary, in no uncertain terms, that she must let him rule in her name.

Almost as soon as she had arrived in Edinburgh, Scotland's capital, Queen Mary sent messages to Queen Elizabeth, trying to establish friendly relations. Queen Mary's ambassador tried to persuade Queen Elizabeth to name Mary, Queen

England and Scotland

England and Scotland had been rivals and enemies for generations. There had been long and bloody wars along the Anglo-Scottish border. In 1503, Princess Margaret of England (Elizabeth's aunt) went north to marry King James IV of Scotland. The marriage was intended to create an alliance between the Thistle and the Rose, as Scotland and England were sometimes known.

Princess Margaret, now Queen Margaret, had a son who became King James V, of Scotland. He died in 1543, and the crown passed to his two-week-old daughter Mary. She spent little of her youth in Scotland, but was instead raised and educated in France. For a time, she and her friends hoped that she would one day become queen of France, Scotland, and England, all at once.

Instead, Mary, Queen of Scots lost her Scottish throne and was confined in an English castle. Meanwhile, her son became King James VI, of Scotland. King James showed little interest in his mother, whom he hardly knew. Instead, he cultivated good relations with Queen Elizabeth. When the queen died in 1603, the English throne passed to James, her first cousin twice removed.

of Scots as her successor, in light of the fact that Queen Elizabeth was not yet married and had no children to serve as heirs to the throne. Queen Elizabeth replied, "More do adore the rising than the setting sun." [13]

She did not want to appoint Queen Mary, or anyone else, as her heir. The English people might then transfer their affections from her to this new person. No, Queen Elizabeth would not name Mary, Queen of Scots as her successor.

In 1563, Queen Elizabeth actually proposed that her dear friend Robert Dudley might be a possible suitor for Queen Mary. The suggestion was rejected, both by the Scots and by Robert Dudley. He did not want to leave England for the far-off land to the north. Then another person presented himself: Lord Darnley.

Darnley was an English Catholic nobleman. Queen Elizabeth thought it would be an excellent idea to marry him off to Mary, Queen of Scots. Darnley went north and quickly charmed Queen Mary, for she was an impetuous woman. She married Darnley, who turned out to be a bully, a bit of a drunk, and a power-hungry man.

Lord Darnley (left) was an English Catholic nobleman who charmed Queen Mary (right). Lord Darnley and Queen Mary eventually married, but it was an unhappy marriage.

Queen Mary soon turned against her husband and found a new favorite. One night, as she and this new favorite man sat down to dinner, Lord Darnley burst into the chamber, pulled out his knife, and killed his rival in front of the queen. As if this were not bad enough, sometime later, Lord Darnley was killed by a gunpowder explosion at his house.

Queen Mary had made a terrible mess of her kingdom. Her Scottish subjects were Protestants and they did not want her. The Scottish lords did not want her because she had shown such bad judgment in marrying Lord Darnley. Queen Mary had no friends and nowhere to turn.

A nobleman named Bothwell came to her rescue. He and the queen married quickly and fought against an uprising of the Scottish nobles. Bothwell and Queen Mary lost the fight and they had to be separated. He went into exile on the continent of Europe and she crossed the border into England. Though she was in her 30s, Queen Mary had never set foot in England before.

Queen Mary hoped that Queen Elizabeth, her first cousin once removed, would be kind and would help her. Queen Mary wrote to Queen Elizabeth, asking for help defeating the rebellion of the Scottish nobles. Queen Elizabeth wrote back, saying that Queen Mary was under suspicion of murder and that she must be held in confinement until the facts were known. This confinement would not be painful or uncomfortable. Queen Mary was allowed to ride her horse and to spend much time outdoors, but she was, for all intents and purposes, a prisoner.

Queen Mary was indignant. This was not right, for one queen to imprison another. Letters went back and forth between Queen Elizabeth and Queen Mary, with Queen Mary always asking for better treatment and freedom. Queen Elizabeth grew quite sharp in her answers. On one occasion she answered:

> Madame:
>
> Of late times I have received diverse letter from you. . . . But now, finding by your last letter of the 27th of the last month, an increase of your impatience tending also to many uncomely, passionate, and vindictive speeches, I thought to change my former opinion.[14]

This was not good news. When a king or queen changed his or her opinion, it could have dire consequences. "I will not by way of letter write any more of the matter, but have rather chosen to commit to my cousin the Earl of Shrewsbury the things which I have thought meet."[15] Lord

Queen Mary (shown here) was imprisoned by her cousin Queen Elizabeth on suspicion of murder. Queen Mary was deeply offended that her cousin, and fellow queen, would imprison her.

Shrewsbury was Queen Mary's jailor. He decided how long she could ride, how much time she could spend outdoors, and how much time she had to be under the watch of her guards. Queen Elizabeth closed the letter by saying, "Your cousin that wisheth you a better mind." [16] Clearly, being a king's or queen's cousin was not always a positive thing.

Test Your Knowledge

1 How old was Mary when she became queen of France?

a. 14

b. 16

c. 12

d. 18

2 How did the king of France die?

a. In a jousting accident

b. On a horse, in a riding accident

c. In a hunting accident

d. As a result of illness

3 How old was Mary when she became a widow?

a. 20

b. 15

c. 17

d. 19

4 Where was Mary born?

a. France

b. England

c. Scotland

d. Spain

5 Lord Shrewsbury was Queen Mary's

a. advisor.

b. jailor.

c. husband.

d. horse trainer.

ANSWERS: 1. b; 2. a; 3. d; 4. c; 5. b

Catholic Versus Protestant

The division between Catholics and Protestants was the single greatest issue of Queen Elizabeth's time, but the trouble between the two groups had actually begun earlier in the century. When Princess Elizabeth became queen in 1558, she affirmed that England was a Protestant nation.

When Philip II became king of Spain in 1556, he affirmed that Spain was a Catholic nation. This included the Dutch Netherlands, which had been part of the Spanish Empire for some time. The Dutch people, who were Protestants, wanted to overthrow the rule of King Philip II. In 1568, they rebelled against Philip II of Spain.

Queen Elizabeth and King Philip knew each other. He had married her half sister Mary in 1554, and she remembered him from his time in England. There was never any personal dislike between Queen Elizabeth and King Philip, but their positions as leaders of major Protestant and Catholic nations led them toward war with each other.

In the 1560s, Queen Elizabeth began to grant commissions to some of her subjects. These commissions allowed the queen's subjects to attack Spanish towns and ships in the New World, but not in the Old World. This was a tricky situation because Elizabeth wanted to stay at peace officially, while secretly making political strides. These commissions made some of her subjects into privateers. Somewhat different from pirates, privateers had an official commission from the government.

Philip II became the king of Spain in 1556. He affirmed Spain's standing as a Catholic nation.

The first two men to receive commissions were John Hawkins and Francis Drake. They were distant cousins and they lived in England's southwestern end, in the county of Devon. Both men were adventurers and they wanted to sail to the New World. Queen Elizabeth granted them commissions as privateers and as captains of slave ships. Yes, the queen—who was greatly admired by her people—authorized men to go to Africa and take people away as slaves. Queen Elizabeth was the first queen to enter into this terrible business, and John Hawkins was her first subject to do the same.

John Hawkins and Francis Drake sailed in 1567. They went to Africa and obtained slaves, whether through trade or kidnapping, and then headed for what we now know as the Caribbean Sea. Hawkins and Drake later landed in Mexico, which was ruled by Spain at the time, and attempted to trade. While they were in the harbor at San Juan de Uloa, the Spanish viceroy appeared with a large fleet of ships. He and John Hawkins drew up an agreement that said the two sides would leave each other alone in the harbor, but the Spanish fleet broke their word. They attacked the English fleet, killing many sailors.

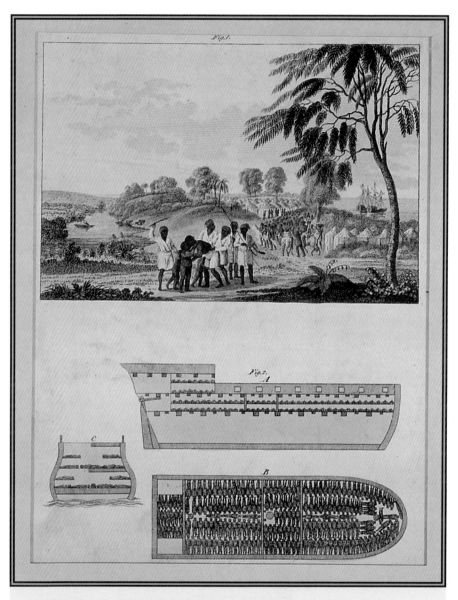

In addition to exploring, Sir John Hawkins and Sir Francis Drake were captains of slave ships. They sailed to Africa to obtain slaves for England. Plans of a slave ship and an illustration of a slave camp are shown here.

Hawkins and Drake were both lucky to get away, and they sailed back to England. The Spanish fleet had been victorious, but their win would cost them very dearly in the future. Both John Hawkins and Francis Drake became lifetime enemies of King Philip and the people of Spain.

On their next voyages, John Hawkins and Francis Drake were luckier. This time, they split up. John Hawkins raided Spanish colonies in the Caribbean, while Francis Drake sailed south—much further south. He had an ambition, a desire. He wanted to be the first Englishman to sail completely around the world.

Today people routinely travel around the world in airplanes and, if they do not stop very often, they can make the journey in a very short time. In the 1570s, only one ship had ever gone completely around the globe. The Spanish ship *Victoria* had encircled the globe between 1519 and 1522. The ship and its crew experienced great hardship. The captain did not live to see the end of the journey. He died in a battle with native people in the Philippine Islands.

Spain had claimed most of the land and the waters of the New World, and the Pacific Ocean, as a result

of this voyage, some 60 years earlier, but Francis
Drake intended to prove Spain wrong. In 1577,
Francis Drake and his crew aboard the *Pelican* sailed
south. They went past Colombia, Brazil, and even
Argentina. They were looking for the famous strait that
Captain Ferdinand Magellan had discovered in 1520.

The Slave Trade

The Portuguese were the first to enter into the
slave trade, a vicious and profitable business.
Having pioneered the way to West Africa, they
started the awful business of enslaving people
and selling them for the highest possible price.
The Portuguese were followed by the Spanish, the
French, the Dutch, and the English. Almost every
European country that had ships, eventually ended
up in the slave trade because it was so profitable.
Some people claim that half of the wealth of
Europe was built on the slave trade.

Ships left England, France, or Spain and sailed to
West Africa. Once there, the shipmasters made deals
with the coastal rulers. The coastal leaders let the
English, French, or Spanish slave traders go inland
and kidnap large numbers of people, who were then
dragged, kicking and screaming, to the coast. Some

Magellan was actually Portuguese, but he had sailed for the king of Spain. He and the crew of the *Victoria* had found the Strait of Magellan. It lies at the bottom of South America, and daring ships and sailors can pass through it to get from the Atlantic Ocean to the Pacific. No Englishman had ever

slaves jumped in the water and drowned themselves, rather than be put in irons and forcibly placed on slave ships.

The slave ships sailed on what we now call the Middle Passage, from West Africa to the Caribbean or parts of South America. Very few of the early ships went to North America, but this number increased as time went on. Most of the some 30 million African Americans of today are descendants of the 550,000 slaves who were forcibly removed from Africa.

Some people who engaged in the terrible practice of slavery, later regretted it. John Newton was a slave-ship captain who later repented. He became a minister in London and wrote the song "Amazing Grace" to describe his conversion from slave trader to humanitarian.

done this. Even the Spanish explorers were very cautious about the traveling through the Strait of Magellan. They preferred to sail all the way up to Panama and send things back and forth across the narrow Isthmus of Panama.

Francis Drake and his men were daring sailors. They found the Strait of Magellan and entered it. Remember, they were the first Englishmen ever to sail through it and they had no maps or charts. They could only use the stories they had heard from Spanish sailors to guide them. Sailors love to brag and boast about what they have done. Therefore communication between English and Spanish people occurred only in an informal way, through exaggerated stories.

As Francis Drake and his men forged ahead, they passed great headlands, points of usually high land jutting out into the water, and frightening blocks of ice. Still, they sailed on through the cold and emerged on the other side. They were the first Englishmen to reach the Pacific Ocean.

Once he was on the Pacific side, Francis Drake attacked Spanish ships and towns. The Spanish people were astonished because they had never seen Englishmen there before. Drake was able to pillage, plunder, and take treasure away from the shocked Spaniards. Around this time, the Spanish people started calling Drake *El Draque*. They believed he had supernatural powers that allowed him to accomplish all that he had undertaken.

Francis Drake and his men sailed up to what is now California. They spent some time around San Francisco Bay, plugging holes and repairing their ship, before setting out across the great Pacific Ocean. They were the first Englishmen to sail all the way across the Pacific and the first to sail through the Indian Ocean. By now, their deeds had won them great acclaim and attention. At home, the English people were cheering for them. The Spaniards on the ocean were trying to catch them, but Drake and his men were out of reach as they sailed around the Cape of Good Hope, at the southern tip of Africa. When it was time to head home to England, Drake arrived to one of the greatest homecomings ever seen.

All of England went wild over the news of Francis Drake's accomplishments. Drake had done things no other Englishman had even tried. He had beaten the Spaniards many times. He had circled the globe and, most importantly, he brought home great treasures in silver and gold.

Queen Elizabeth was as pleased with Francis Drake's accomplishment as were her people. She admired Francis Drake and what he had done, but she had to be careful. The ambassador from Spain was demanding that the treasure Francis Drake had claimed be returned. He was also demanding Francis Drake's head. Only when these two demands were met would peace be maintained between Spain and England.

Of course, England and Spain were fighting against each other in the Netherlands and on the great oceans, but these were undeclared wars. They were being fought secretly, without declarations of war by either country. If Queen Elizabeth wanted to keep some type of peace with Spain, any type, she would have to turn Francis Drake over to Spain, but Queen Elizabeth could not do this. So, she pretended to care about what the Spanish ambassador said. She also listened to what her people said, but, in keeping with her trademark style, she made up her own mind.

In the spring of 1581, Queen Elizabeth boarded Francis Drake's ship. It was anchored in the Thames River, in London. The ship had been called the *Pelican*, but Drake had renamed it the *Golden Hind*, in honor of all the treasure he brought home. Queen Elizabeth noticed how small the ship was. She marveled at the fact that such a small ship could sail around the world. She called for Francis Drake, who came and bowed before her.

Queen Elizabeth first scolded him. She reminded him of how much trouble he had caused between England and Spain. Then, she turned to her side and had a sword brought forth. She raised it and tapped him lightly, first on his right shoulder and then on his left, knighting him Sir Francis Drake.

Test Your Knowledge

1   What was the single greatest issue of Queen
    Elizabeth's time?
    a. The great divide between the rich and
       the poor
    b. The fact that she and her half sister
       Queen Mary did not get along
    c. The fact that she never married
    d. The division between Protestants and Catholics

2   How did privateers differ from pirates?
    a. Privateers had an official commission
       from the queen.
    b. Privateers worked on land, not at sea.
    c. Privateers did not steal things.
    d. Privateers were hired by individuals.

3   Queen Elizabeth was the first queen to enter
    what business?
    a. Gold mining
    b. The slave trade
    c. Winemaking
    d. Farming

4   In the 1570s, only one ship had done what?
    a. Sailed to Asia
    b. Sailed with a complete crew of men
    c. Gone completely around the globe
    d. Sailed to Africa

5 Sir Francis Drake and his men were the first
to reach

a. Africa.

b. Asia.

c. the Atlantic Ocean.

d. the Pacific Ocean.

ANSWERS: 1. d; 2. a; 3. b; 4. c; 5. d

The Thunder Clouds of War

King Philip and the Spanish ambassador were both very upset. Queen Elizabeth had shown great favor to Francis Drake, the worst privateer of them all. The 1580s were a tense time. Queen Elizabeth was more loved by her people than ever before, but she still faced many dangers. One of those dangers was just across the English Channel in Holland.

The Dutch people had been fighting for their independence since 1568. The people of the Netherlands and Spain hated each other and the war between them had become quite cruel. King Philip sent a great army to try to conquer the Netherlands. The Spaniards were terrific soldiers and they had a wonderful leader in the Duke of Parma. He won many victories and slowly tried to smother the Dutch independence movement.

Queen Elizabeth was very frightened. She believed that, if King Philip and the Duke of Parma captured all of the Netherlands, they would turn on England next. So, in the 1580s, she sent large sums of money to help the Dutch rebels. She did not want to see them crushed by the strength of Spain.

In the mid-1580s, Queen Elizabeth sent her oldest friend, Robert Dudley, to help the Dutch. He was a little over 50 years old and no longer as handsome and dashing as he had been, but he was still a very brave man. Landing in the Netherlands, Robert Dudley brought the English and Dutch forces together to fight against the Spaniards.

The Spaniards tried to conquer the Netherlands under the leadership of Alessandro Farnese, the Duke of Parma. He was an influential leader who won many victories against the Dutch independence movement.

There was also danger on the high seas. Queen Elizabeth was very proud of what Sir Francis Drake had accomplished. He had been the first Englishman to sail around the world and he and his men had done great damage to the Spanish treasure fleets, but the attacks by Francis Drake served only to increase the resolve of the Spanish forces. In the 1580s, King Philip II built up the Spanish navy, making it larger and greater than ever before. It seemed likely that he would turn against England at some point in the future.

Meanwhile, Queen Elizabeth had only the Dutch rebels as allies. As a queen who believed that it was God's will for kings and queens to rule, she disliked the Dutch rebels. After all, they were fighting against their lawful king, Philip II. As a ruler and a clever politician, however, she knew that she had to remain on good terms with the Dutch rebels. After all, they were her only allies. She thought about trying to make an ally of Catholic France, but that effort failed. By the middle of the 1580s, England was very much alone in a world in which the forces of Catholicism were gaining strength. The pope, who admired Elizabeth as a person, thought she should be ejected from her throne. He offered King Philip of Spain one million ducats in gold the day the first Spanish soldiers landed on English soil.

One million ducats was a generous offer, but King Philip had other, even better reasons to invade. He and his counselors were convinced that Queen Elizabeth's aid to the Dutch rebels was

The Dutch Revolt

In 1568, at the start of a very long war for independence, the people of Holland and Zeeland—provinces in the northern part of the Netherlands—rose up against Spain. The rebellion lasted, off and on, until 1648. The people of Holland and Zeeland were accustomed to sailing the seas and trading with many other nations. They rose up in revolt when King Philip of Spain tried to make their lands more like those of the Spanish Empire.

Spain had far more trained men and more ships than the Dutch, but the Dutch ships were better built. As time passed, it became clear that Holland and Zeeland would not be easy to conquer. These two little provinces were surrounded by the North Sea on one side and marshes, rivers, and dikes on the other keeping the rebels strong. If King Philip could conquer England, he would solve three problems at once: his rivalry with Elizabeth, the attacks her privateers made, and the Dutch revolt. Yet, King Philip was hesitant to act. He recognized the English strength at sea and he knew the English people loved their queen. Even with all of the provocations Queen Elizabeth had instigated, King

side. The Dutch were master builders of dikes and they defended them masterfully, too.

Perhaps King Philip could have won if he could have concentrated his forces. At that time, however, Spain was committed on many different fronts. Spanish forces battled the Turks in the Mediterranean, the English in the New World, and the Dutch in Holland. These battles depleted Spanish forces and cost Spain a great deal of money.

King Philip died in 1598, but his son and grandson kept up the struggle. Only in 1648, with the Treaty of Munster, was the issue finally settled. Holland, Zeeland, and five other provinces became the United Provinces of the Netherlands.

Philip still needed one overwhelming reason to invade England—and he obtained it in the winter of 1587.

Meanwhile, Queen Mary had continued to be an annoyance to Queen Elizabeth. The Scottish queen still lived in captivity, but she now had a harsh man as her jailor. The Scottish queen was aging quickly because she could not ride and exercise as she liked. All of her pleas to Elizabeth for better treatment had gone unheeded.

Queen Elizabeth was not generally known to be cruel, but she could be ruthless. Any sympathy or kind treatment she offered her cousin Queen Mary might simply encourage the people who wanted to create a Catholic uprising in Mary's name. England was now largely Protestant, but there were still enough Catholics around to create quite a stir. There were also rumors of plots to kill Queen Elizabeth and replace her with Mary, Queen of Scots.

Francis Walsingham, the chief of Queen Elizabeth's spies, laid a trap for Mary, Queen of Scots. Two men employed by Walsingham approached her, saying they would smuggle messages out of the castle where she was being held prisoner. Thinking she had a new opportunity, Queen Mary sent many letters out of the castle. All of them were read by Walsingham and his spies. The letters confirmed that Queen Mary had, indeed, plotted to kill Queen Elizabeth, and Walsingham took the letters to his queen.

Queen Elizabeth was not pleased. Of course, she was upset to learn that her cousin had been plotting to kill her, but she was also upset that Walsingham had laid this trap without consulting her. Queen Elizabeth was now in a very difficult position. If she allowed Queen Mary to live, there would surely be future plots. If she had Queen Mary executed, she would be setting a very bad example. No good king or queen wanted to have another royal killed. People might get the idea that it was acceptable to attack and kill royalty.

Queen Elizabeth did not like the predicament in which she found herself. She was angry with Walsingham for bringing the information to her. She was also angry with members of her privy council, who agreed that the Scottish queen must die. Most of all, Elizabeth was angry that the situation had ever come this far. A trial had taken place earlier

When Queen Elizabeth found out that her cousin Mary, Queen of Scots had been plotting to kill her, Queen Elizabeth had Mary executed.

and Queen Mary had been found guilty. Finally, in February 1587, Queen Elizabeth signed the warrant for the queen's execution. Days later, however, Queen Elizabeth changed her mind. She did not want her cousin to be killed, but it was too late. Knowing that the queen might change her mind, her privy council had made sure the execution was carried out at once. Mary, Queen of Scots went to her death bravely. The executioner took two swings with the axe to kill her.

Queen Elizabeth had rid herself of a terrible danger, but she was about to experience something even worse. As soon as he learned of the death of Queen Mary, King Philip declared war on England. He told the pope and other European leaders that he would send men to England to conquer the land, which would be returned to the Roman Catholic faith.

Test Your Knowledge

1 Since when had the Dutch been fighting for their independence?

    a. 1658

    b. 1558

    c. 1568

    d. 1685

2 Why did Queen Elizabeth help the Dutch rebels?

    a. Because she was a good friend to the leader of Holland

    b. Because she believed that Spain would attack England next

    c. Because she always supported those in need of help

    d. Because she wanted to test her military powers

3 What did Queen Mary plan to do?

    a. Kill Queen Elizabeth

    b. Become ruler of England

    c. Become ruler of Scotland

    d. Marry Francis Walsingham

4 As soon as he learned of the death of Queen Mary, King Philip

    a. declared war on Scotland.

    b. went to England to comfort Queen Elizabeth.

    c. declared war on France.

    d. declared war on England.

5 King Philip wanted to

a. return England to the Roman Catholic faith.

b. marry Queen Elizabeth.

c. create an alliance between England and Spain.

d. merge the Spanish and English armed forces.

ANSWERS: 1. c; 2. b; 3. a; 4. d; 5. a

The Preemptive Strike

The time had come for King Philip to launch his fleet of ships, known as the Spanish Armada, against England. Spanish sailors and soldiers were busy building new ships and fixing old ones. They brought supplies of wine and meat on board their ships. They were getting ready to sail, but Queen Elizabeth had Sir Francis Drake on her side.

Not only had he gone all the way around the world, but Drake had also terrorized the Spaniards. They believed he was a great magician who had a magic mirror. Using this mirror, they thought he could see around the curves of land and ocean, and he could see Spanish ships coming from far away. This was the only way they could explain his amazing successes.

As soon as he learned that the Spanish fleet was about to set sail, Sir Francis Drake went before Queen Elizabeth. He begged her to allow him to attack the Spanish fleet in their home ports. By taking the war to Spain, he could prevent, or at least delay, the fleet from sailing.

Queen Elizabeth hesitated. Throughout her life and her reign as queen, she had always done best by waiting. She was a master of waiting and letting her opponent make the first move, but there was no time for that now. If she was going to strike, she must do it now. She gave Francis Drake a commission and he went on his way.

Knowing the queen's tendency to change her mind, Francis Drake sailed at once and it was lucky he did, for Queen Elizabeth quickly sent a second message. This time, she forbade him to enter the ports of Spain, but it was too late. Drake had already sailed from Plymouth.

Francis Drake sailed down through the Bay of Biscay. He sailed past Portugal and dipped around the southwest corner of Europe. He passed by the Portuguese port of Lisbon. It was well defended, both by Spanish forces and by nature. When he sailed into the harbor at Cadiz, Spain, however, there was nothing to stop him.

Cadiz was the largest Spanish port. It had been a port since Roman times, maybe even longer than that. The Spanish fleet had collected vast numbers of ships, men, and supplies here. They should have been watching. They should have had lookouts, but they expected to sail and attack the English, not to be attacked by them. When Francis Drake sailed into the harbor at Cadiz, the Spaniards were in a panic.

Men ran. Sailors fled. People abandoned their ships, while Francis Drake and his men took

Francis Drake (shown here) surprised the Spaniards when he sailed into the harbor at Cadiz, Spain, to attack the Spanish Armada. The Spanish fleet had been expecting to lead the attack on England.

valuable possessions and burned other things. Ropes, sails, even entire ships went up in flames. Francis Drake was in the thick of the fight, but the battle was easy because the Spaniards were so panicked and surprised.

Drake might even have captured the town. He was about to lead his men ashore when a Spanish commander, the Duke of Medina Sedonia, appeared. He and his musketeers drove the English away from the shore. After 24 hours of burning and pillaging, Francis Drake sailed away. He had destroyed 24 Spanish ships of different sizes. He had set back the plans of the Spanish Armada by months, maybe even more. Most important, he had instilled terrible fear in the Spaniards. They dreaded this man they called *El Draque.*

Francis Drake was not finished conquering. He sailed away from Spain and headed toward Portugal. He captured the tiny town of Sagres, located on the extreme southwest end of Portugal. From there, he could attack the ships of either Spain or Portugal, no matter which direction they headed. He had done an amazing thing. He had isolated the Spanish from their Portuguese allies.

King Philip of Spain was furious. Francis Drake had a way of making a mess of his plans. King Philip was upset that his ships did not sail out from Lisbon to fight Drake. Instead, the Spanish and Portuguese forces stayed safe in the snug harbor. They did not wish to meet Drake out on the open sea.

Francis Drake stayed in Portuguese waters for a month. He sailed by Lisbon many times. He taunted the Spaniards, asking them to come out and fight. When they would not do so, Drake finally sailed for home. Like any good sailor, first he filled up his casks with water and loaded his ship with fresh food.

Upon his return to Plymouth, Francis Drake became a national hero. His name was on everyone's lips. He had done such incredible things. Queen Elizabeth did not remind Drake that she had sent a second order to stop him. She did not tell him that he should not have attacked the Spanish forces in their ports. She was grateful for what he had done. He had given her time in which to prepare to meet the Spanish Armada.

The Spaniards had to put off their attack for a full year. It would take them that long to repair the damage Francis Drake had done. Queen Elizabeth used that year to increase the size of her army. She brought back soldiers who had gone to the Netherlands. Most of all, she improved the English navy. Because Sir Francis Drake had "bought her time," Queen Elizabeth was able to have more frigates built. Throughout the fall and winter of 1587, the English built more ships. They knew the Spaniards were doing the same.

During the winter of 1587, King Philip developed his master plan. He no longer had Queen Mary as an ally, but that was just fine. He had other plans and other hopes. Spanish forces had conquered most, but not all, of the Netherlands. The Spanish soldiers were close to the English Channel and they wanted to conquer England.

Under the master plan, the Spanish Armada would sail from Cadiz up to England and squeeze into the narrow English Channel. The galleons and galleys of the fleet would pick up the Spanish army in the Netherlands. Those soldiers would then be ferried across the channel and would land in England.

This was a bold plan. It had strategy, but, like many good plans, it would need almost perfect

Sir Francis Drake's surprise attack allowed Queen Elizabeth time to increase the size of the English army. She also had more frigates built (like the one shown here).

timing. The Spanish soldiers in the Netherlands would have to be on the shore at exactly the right moment, in order to be picked up. The Spanish

Armada would have to sail at just the right moment and arrive just in time.

King Philip knew the dangers. He knew that there might be obstacles, but he believed that God was on his side. He ordered the Spanish fleet to sail under the command of the Duke of Medina Sedonia. The duke was a good and courageous man. He was from the highest level of the Spanish nobility, but he was not a sailor. He had seldom gone to sea and usually got seasick when he did. The duke told all of this to King Philip, but the king brushed aside these fears. Go, he said, and conquer England. He believed that God was with the Spanish fleet and that all would be well.

The Spanish Armada sailed out of Cadiz in the spring of 1588, with about 130 ships carrying some 30,000 men. The ships made a brave and beautiful sight. Many of them had pictures of Roman Catholic saints painted on their sails. The Spanish ships sailed up the west side of Portugal. By the time they reached the northern part, where Spain and Portugal meet, many of the men were seasick. The fleet entered the port of Corunna, where the

Different Kinds of Ships

Since the time of Christopher Columbus, galleons and galleys had been typical sailing ships. The large and heavy galleons could carry many men and a great deal of cargo. The galleys, powered by slaves who rowed with oars, were light and could turn from side to side very quickly. Both the galleons and the galleys had been perfected by Spanish sailors, who sailed in both the Mediterranean Sea and the Atlantic Ocean, and needed both kinds of ships.

The English forces did not sail in the Mediterranean. Nearly all of their ships were in the North Sea, the English Channel, or the Atlantic Ocean. They needed a different kind of ship. Under Queen Elizabeth, the English developed the frigate, a lighter, sleeker ship than the galleon. The frigate could turn around almost as fast as the galley, but it was powered by sails and ropes, not by slaves using oars. The frigate used the speed of the galley and added some of the strength of the galleon.

Spanish ships stayed for two weeks, loading up on fresh water and supplies.

Meanwhile, the Spanish army in the Netherlands was waiting. The Spanish soldiers were eager to get on with the fight. They did not know why their fleet still had not arrived. At the same time, Queen Elizabeth gathered her forces. She loved and admired Sir Francis Drake, but he had only recently been made a knight. She gave the top command to Thomas Howard, Lord of Effingham. Drake was the number two or number three man in command. The English frigates waited at Plymouth for a sign of the Spanish Armada.

The Spaniards took a long time to arrive. When news first arrived that the Spanish fleet had been sighted, Sir Francis Drake and his captains were playing a game of bowls, similar to croquet. Everyone was very excited and nervous, but Sir Francis Drake said, "Time enough to finish the game and beat the Spaniards after." [17] This wonderful confidence was why men liked Sir Francis Drake. They felt that, with him leading, things would go well.

Drake and his captains finished the game before they rowed out to their ships. By evening, the whole English fleet was out on the open sea. When morning came, the two fleets saw each other. Each was amazed and a little frightened by the other, but ready to do battle.

Test Your Knowledge

1 King Philip's fleet of ships was known as

  a. the Spanish Fleet.

  b. the Spanish Flotilla.

  c. the Spanish Armada.

  d. the Spanish Navy.

2 After conquering Spain, Sir Francis Drake headed toward

  a. Portugal.

  b. Italy.

  c. France.

  d. Africa.

3 How many ships were in the Spanish fleet?

  a. 200

  b. 30

  c. 100

  d. 130

4 Bowls was a game similar to

  a. bowling.

  b. croquet.

  c. tennis.

  d. soccer.

5 Men liked Sir Francis Drake because

a. he was confident.

b. he was a good sailor.

c. he was a skilled navigator.

d. he was kind to everyone.

ANSWERS: 1. c; 2. a; 3. d; 4. b; 5. a

The Spanish Armada

The English fleet had about 100 ships. Many were frigates, but there were also some galleons. Some coastal fishing ships had also been drafted into the English navy. The Spanish fleet had about 130 ships. Ten ships, however, had already been swept away by storms and sickness. The Spanish fleet consisted of a combination of galleons and galleys. To make them look even more menacing, the Spaniards arranged their ships in the shape of a crescent, or a half moon. This vast group of ships was slowly drifting toward England.

Lord Thomas Howard and Sir Francis Drake attacked first. As the English ships came sailing down on the Spanish fleet, the wind was behind their backs, allowing the English forces to attack at will. Cannonballs sailed through the air. Muskets thundered. Pikes (spears) and cutlasses (swords) swished through the air. The Spanish fleet was ready. Soldiers were ready to board the English ships and attack. The English fleet would not come too close. Their ships stayed about half a cannon shot away and continued to fire at the Spanish ships.

The Spanish soldiers wanted to come close, to board and fight hand to hand, but the English forces, which had the faster ships, would not let them. Instead, the English gunners continued firing, making a great deal of noise. The fighting went on all day. By the time night came, the Spanish fleet had taken a great deal of damage, but their mighty crescent formation was still in place.

English ships, under the direction of Lord Thomas Howard and Sir Francis Drake, attacked first. The sea battle between the Spanish Armada and English naval forces is shown here.

By the morning of the second day, the two fleets had drifted east. They were near the Isle of Wight, off England's south coast. When the fighting started again, the Spanish forces kept trying to come close, but the English ships maintained their distance. Cannons roared on both sides.

On his flagship, the Duke of Medina Sedonia was worried. He knew that he had to reach the Spanish soldiers in the Netherlands. He also knew that his supply of gunpowder was running low. Of all the things the Spaniards had packed, gunpowder was in shortest supply. Cannonballs and gunpowder took up a lot of room and there were only 80 rounds left for each Spanish gun.

At one point, several English frigates teamed up against one Spanish galleon. They were about to capture it when the Duke of Medina Sedonia sailed over in his flagship to rescue the galleon that was in trouble. No one doubted the duke's bravery, but the Spanish Armada was clearly in serious trouble.

On the third day, both sides came together for action, but the wind and waves sent them eastward. All day, it was hard to exchange fire, much less grapple and come aboard, as the Spanish wanted. The battle seemed to be fizzling out.

On the fourth day, the Duke of Medina Sedonia and the Spanish Armada reached the harbor at Calais on French soil, on the east side of the English Channel. The French governor allowed the Spanish ships to anchor there. Now, they had a safe haven—

or so they thought. The duke sent message after message to the Spanish army in the Netherlands. If only the soldiers were here, now, he could pick them up, but even though the Spanish soldiers were only some 50 miles away, they could not get to the coast fast enough. Dutch soldiers also blocked the way.

The English Channel

Certain bodies of water, such as the English Channel, are very important because of their strategic location. The channel marks a narrow separation of water between England on one side and France, Belgium, and Holland on the other. Only 24 miles separate Dover on the English side from Calais on the French side. During Queen Elizabeth's time, people often called the English Channel the "Narrow Seas," and everyone understood the strategic importance of this stretch of water.

Queen Elizabeth wanted control of the channel because it allowed her to protect England from Spain. King Philip wanted the channel because it would enable Spanish forces to attack either England or Holland. The French wanted the channel for

The duke must have realized that there was no way to carry out King Philip's orders, but he was a soldier and a man of honor. He tried to do his duty. All Spanish commanders knew they had to adhere to King Philip's master plan. The Spanish system of government did not allow for people to break free from rules and established systems. Perhaps that

similar reasons. The Dutch wanted the channel because it was their first line of defense against Spain.

Skirmishes for control of the channel went on for many years. Even after Spain was defeated and there was no future threat of Spanish invasions, English, French, and Dutch forces continued to fight for this area. England was again threatened with invasion in the time of Napoleon, when control of the channel proved vital to England's security.

On a lighter note, quite a few people over the centuries have attempted to swim the length of the English Channel, from Dover to Calais or the reverse. Several men did it and the first woman to do so was Gertrude Ederle, who swam the 24 miles in 1923.

accounts for the fact that there was no one like Sir Francis Drake in the Spanish fleet.

While the Spanish ships waited in the harbor, the English captains got together. Lord Howard asked his captains what they thought and everyone looked at Francis Drake. He was the best and the boldest among them. Sir Francis Drake gave his answer. They should not wait, he said, for the Spaniards to do anything. Instead they should attack with fire ships, ships that were lit on fire just before they reached the enemy.

Everyone agreed this was a good, though risky, plan. Eight old ships were brought together and loaded with pitch, tar, and gunpowder. At night, the eight ships were sent toward the Spanish Armada. English sailors stayed on board as long as they could, before lighting their explosives and jumping off the sides of the ships.

Up to this point, the Spanish ships had held together very well. The crescent formation was one of their great strengths. Even though they had taken a pounding from the English cannons, the Spanish ships had stayed in tight formation. The fire ships changed all that.

The Spanish fleet was in a panic. Captain after captain had his men cut the long rope and chain that held his ship's anchor. The Spanish ships generally got out of the way of the fire ships, which burned at the water's edge, but the damage had been done. When dawn came, the Spanish ships were bobbing up and down in the English Channel. Their great crescent formation was completely destroyed. Instead, the Spanish ships were spread out over many miles. Without their anchors, the Spanish ships could not hold their positions. As the wind shifted, some of them drifted dangerously close to the French shore. There were lots of rocks there and the ships were in peril. The English chose this moment to attack.

Sir Francis Drake and Lord Howard led the attack. The English ships where everywhere, surrounding galleys and galleons. The English knew these waters very well and they still had their anchors. So they were able to maneuver while the Spanish ships did their best just to stay put.

Throughout that day, cannons roared. The Spanish and English forces were both very brave, but when night came, the Spanish fleet was completely out of gunpowder. The 80 rounds they had brought from Spain were not enough for such a contest.

The next day, the Spanish captains talked. They could not win the battle here in the English Channel, so they had only two choices. They could either turn toward the south—and try to fight their way home—or they could sail north, head around Scotland and Ireland, and try to get home that way. In the end, the wind made the choice for them when it suddenly shifted direction. The Spanish ships, lacking anchors, could not hold their positions. They were blown north on the first part of their long voyage home.

The English commanders were very happy. They knew that the danger was over. Not only was the Spanish fleet out of gunpowder, but their ships were also being blown far away to the north. Lord Howard and Sir Francis Drake sent messages ashore. The Spanish Armada had been defeated! Before those messages reached land, Queen Elizabeth gave the greatest speech of her life. Knowing that the danger was real, she told her military commanders that she wanted to speak to the troops. On August 9, before she knew that the

Even before learning of the English victory over the Spanish Armada, Queen Elizabeth spoke to her troops at Tilbury. The arrival of Queen Elizabeth at Tilbury and the defeat of the Spanish Armada are depicted here.

wind had shifted, Elizabeth rode into her soldiers' camp at Tilbury.

Queen Elizabeth was now 55 years old. She wore a wig to conceal the bald spots on her head. She moved more slowly now and did not dance as much, but all of these things were forgotten when she rode into Tilbury on a beautiful white horse. She was surrounded by men in armor and she was quite a sight to see.

In her speech, Queen Elizabeth showed scorn for the enemy. She said:

> I am come amongst you . . . being resolved, in the midst and heat of the battle, to live or die amongst you; to lay down for God, my kingdom, and for my people, my honor and my blood, even in the dust. I know I have but the body of a weak and feeble woman; but I have the heart and stomach of a king, and a king of England too.[18]

The men roared. Trumpets blew. The horses shied away from the noise. This was the greatest speech of Queen Elizabeth's long life. It was one of the great speeches in history. She showed, once more, that she would never yield to an enemy.

She was the queen and she would live or die with her people.

Just days later, came the news that the wind had shifted and the Spanish fleet was gone. Queen Elizabeth gave great thanks. A medal was created, showing her proud face on one side and the Spanish ships bobbing up and down on the waves on the other. The medal carried these words, "God breathed, and they were scattered." [19]

Test Your Knowledge

1 The Spaniards arranged their ships in the shape of

a. a circle.

b. an "L."

c. a crescent or half moon.

d. a "T."

2 Of all the things the Spaniards had packed, what was in the shortest supply?

a. Gunpowder

b. Food

c. Water

d. Cannonballs

3 The Spaniards thought they had found a safe haven

a. on Italian soil.

b. on French soil.

c. on English soil.

d. on Scottish soil.

4 The Spanish soldiers in the Netherlands were only about how many miles away?

a. 60

b. 40

c. 35

d. 50

5 How many fire ships did the English use?

a. Eight

b. Four

c. Three

d. Five

ANSWERS: 1. c; 2. a; 3. b; 4. d; 5. a

Queen Elizabeth and Her Court

Queen Elizabeth and the English fleet had emerged victorious, while the Spanish forces headed home in defeat. The ships of the Spanish Armada had a terrible time on their way home. They sailed around Scotland and Ireland in the beginning of the autumn, an awful time in those waters. Many ships ran aground off the coast of Ireland, and many men either drowned or were killed when they came ashore. The results were disastrous. By the time they made it back to Spain, the Spanish forces had lost about half of their men and ships.

King Philip of Spain was very disappointed. His grand Armada had come to nothing, but he was not angry with the Duke of Medina Sedonia. If anything, the duke had done better than many other men would have. The duke returned to his lands and lived as a country gentleman.

King Philip did not give up on his desire to conquer England. Twice more he collected ships and fleets, but weather prevented either fleet from reaching England. By the middle of the 1590s, it was clear that Spain could not conquer England. As the danger from Spain faded, Queen Elizabeth paid more attention to her court and her nobles. She even paid some attention to the New World.

Queen Elizabeth had always dressed well. She had also danced well. Now, in the last decade of the 1500s, she put on an even greater show than ever. She always wore beautiful clothes, decked out with jewels. When she met foreign ambassadors,

With the threat of attack from Spain gone, Queen Elizabeth was able turn her attention to her court. The queen always wore beautiful clothing and was known as the greatest queen of her time.

they were amazed by her knowledge. She had become the greatest queen, perhaps the greatest monarch, of her time.

Sadly, during this time, Queen Elizabeth lost her only real love. She had never married Robert Dudley, the Earl of Leicester, but she had always loved him. He died of natural causes the same year that the English fleet defeated the Spanish Armada.

By now, Queen Elizabeth, who had never married, was called the Virgin Queen. She was famous the world over. As her looks faded, however, she sometimes became jealous of her maids of honor, a group of young women who paid close attention to the queen. They helped her dress, bathe, and attend to all manner of personal hygiene issues. A maid of honor could not marry unless the queen agreed to it, but Queen Elizabeth was so jealous and so suspicious of her maids that some of them married in secret. This caused terrible commotion in the royal court.

Queen Elizabeth knew she would never marry. If she had ever been willing, that time had passed. She was very sad, but she was the queen. She could not be sad for long, or her people would lose heart. So she kept up her style at court and new, younger men were attracted to her. One of those men was Sir Walter Raleigh. He came from southwestern England and was the son of a gentleman farmer. It is said that, the first time Walter Raleigh met Queen Elizabeth, the weather was rainy. According to the story, there were puddles of rain on the ground. Walter Raleigh is said to have taken off his new cloak and laid it over one of the puddles, so the queen could pass by. This was the kind of attention she loved and Walter Raleigh quickly became one of her favorites.

Another favorite with the queen was the Earl of Essex. Like Walter Raleigh, he was a handsome young man. She liked to joke and laugh with both of her favorites. When they claimed they loved her, she would laugh and say they were acting silly over an old woman.

Sir Walter Raleigh was very interested in America. He persuaded the queen to let him try to colonize there. There were many Native Americans in North America, but almost no Europeans. There were only a handful of Spanish colonists in northern Florida. Sir Walter Raleigh sent the first boat-loads of English settlers over to North America in 1585. They sailed from England and landed off the coast of North Carolina. This was a beautiful area because of the woods, sandy beaches, birds, and animals. It was part of the migration zones for birds, and there were many beautiful sounds in the area.

The English colonists landed on one of the islands there. They built some houses and a fort. Soon, they met the local Native Americans. The natives seemed friendly, at first, and things went well for the new colony. The settlers called their new colony Roanoke.

Good things and bad things sometimes come together in batches. This was certainly true at the colony of Roanoke. The beautiful sounds and the lovely birds and animals showed that this was a migration zone. It seemed like a good place for the English to be, but the wind and the waves also showed that this was a geographic zone, a place where different tides and currents come together. Today we know this to be true because terrible hurricanes come up from the Caribbean and strike this area. The settlers were very close to Cape Hatteras, one of the most dangerous areas on the Atlantic coast.

The English ships sailed away, leaving the colonists on this dangerous shore. Over the next year, the colonists and the Native Americans started to fight. By the time a group of supply ships came back, most of the colonists were eager to leave. To their surprise, they found that the supply ships were led by Sir Francis Drake. Drake took the settlers home, and they were very pleased to see England again. In the meantime, however, another boatload of settlers landed at Roanoke Island. They were surprised and frightened to see that the former settlement had been abandoned. They settled down, rebuilt the houses, and planned for the future, but they would soon mysteriously disappear.

Queen Elizabeth knew about the 100 or so settlers at Roanoke, but it was not her job to care for them. That was Sir Walter Raleigh's job. After all, he had sent them there in the first place. As it turned out, neither the queen nor Walter Raleigh could do anything for the settlers because this was 1588, the year of the Spanish Armada. All of England's ships and sailors were needed at home. Only after the Spanish Armada was defeated, could the queen turn her attention to America.

Queen Elizabeth was not to blame for the mysterious disappearance of the colonists at Roanoke, but the loss made her time as queen seem less grand than it might have been. Roanoke was one of the few failures of her reign. Sir Walter Raleigh fell from favor because of Roanoke. He was a very clever

Sir Walter Raleigh (shown here) had a great interest in exploring America. He persuaded Queen Elizabeth to allow him to establish colonies in America. In the Roanoke colony in Virginia, all of the settlers would mysteriously disappear.

man and he managed to win back the queen's friendship, but he never regained her close favor.

The Earl of Essex was now the queen's clear favorite. The queen ate with him, danced with him, and seemed happiest when she was with him. Like Sir Walter Raleigh, the Earl of Essex was ambitious. He wanted to make a name for himself, so he asked the queen to let him go to Ireland.

Roanoke, "The Lost Colony"

In 1590, five years after the first settlement was established on Roanoke Island, two ships arrived there with supplies. When the English came ashore, they found buildings still standing, but no people. There were no signs of conflict or war, but not a single colonist was found.

The men from the supply ships walked through the woods. They shouted, called out, even sang English songs, but no one answered. Something very strange was going on. One of the Englishmen found a tree with the words "GONE TO CROATOAN" carved into its bark.

Croatoan Island was not far away, just a little to the south, but as the English supply ships got ready to go to Croatoan, a major storm blew up. Today, the people who live in this area are always on the

Ireland, also known as the Emerald Isle, is lush and green. Its people are very friendly, but, in the time of Queen Elizabeth, England tried to rule Ireland. There were English soldiers there, and landlords too. Both groups tried to dominate the Irish. This led to a series of revolts. The Earl of Essex was sent to Ireland to settle one of the revolts.

alert. Sometimes they have to leave the area during these storms.

The storm was so strong that the English gave up the attempt. They sailed for home, away from the dangerous waters around Roanoke and Croatoan, and left the settlers to their fate. Even today, we do not know what happened to these first settlers. They may have been killed in fighting with the natives, but, if so, where were the bodies? They may have joined with the natives by marrying into their tribe, but no one can prove it. Perhaps they wandered off toward Florida, looking for Spanish settlements in the South. They may have died in the forest somewhere and their bodies were covered up. Even today, Roanoke is known as "The Lost Colony."

Queen Elizabeth was very careful with money. She had always prided herself on her ability to keep the kingdom out of debt. She liked the Earl of Essex so much, however, that she gave him a large army and a great deal of money. He sailed away for Ireland with orders to put down the rebellion. For unknown reasons, the earl did not move quickly. He wasted time all summer and only went on the campaign in the autumn. By then, it was too late to do much of anything, so he signed a truce with the Irish rebels.

Queen Elizabeth was usually very forgiving toward her favorites, but not this time. She wrote to the Earl of Essex and used very strong words. He had not done his duty. He had not accomplished his mission in Ireland. When he got the letter, the Earl of Essex was very worried. He realized that the queen was turning against him, but he remembered that he had always done well with her in person. Without any orders, he sailed for England. He entered London without anyone knowing and went straight to Queen Elizabeth. She was shocked to see him so suddenly and did not know what to do.

Days later, the queen made sure that the Earl of Essex lost some of his favor and funds. Months after that, the earl started a revolt against Queen Elizabeth—the only time in her long reign that one of her nobles had turned against her. The revolt was put down very quickly. The Earl of Essex learned what he should have known before—that the people would never overthrow Queen Elizabeth. They loved her too much.

The Earl of Essex became a prisoner, but Queen Elizabeth had to decide what to do next. She had a very difficult decision to make. Although she was now an old woman, Queen Elizabeth had always loved dashing, gallant men. First, there had been "Robin," the Earl of Leicester. Then Sir Walter Raleigh layed his cloak in the puddles for her. Now the Earl of Essex had failed her.

Queen Elizabeth waited a long time. She hated having to make this decision, but, in the end, there was no choice. The queen's executioner beheaded the Earl of Essex. Queen Elizabeth was now very sad. All of the young, gallant men of her reign seemed to have gone. The joy of ruling, perhaps even the joy of life, was beginning to leave her.

Test Your Knowledge

1 In what season did the defeated Spanish Armada
set sail?
a. Winter
b. Spring
c. Summer
d. Autumn

2 By the time the Spanish fleet made it home, they
had lost about how many of their men and ships?
a. One-third
b. One-half
c. One-quarter
d. Two-thirds

3 Queen Elizabeth, who had never married, was
called the
a. Virgin Queen.
b. Old Maid Queen.
c. Unmarried Queen.
d. Lonely Queen.

4 About how many settlers disappeared from the
Roanoke colony?
a. 50
b. 200
c. 100
d. 25

5 Sir Walter Raleigh fell from favor because of

a. his overly ambitious desires.

b. his lavish spending on expeditions.

c. his inability to discover new lands.

d. the disappearance of the Roanoke colonists.

ANSWERS: 1. d; 2. b; 3. a; 4. c; 5. d

End of the Golden Age

As the year 1599 came to an end, Queen Elizabeth and England entered a new century, the seventeenth. Queen Elizabeth had been in power for 42 years. During that time, her love for her subjects and their love for her had increased. There was a remarkable bond between this ruler and her subjects, something seldom seen in history.

Queen Elizabeth knew, however, that she would not live much longer. One by one, her faithful advisors and friends had died. Perhaps the cruelest loss had been the death of William Cecil, Lord Burghley. He had been at Elizabeth's side through the early days of her rule and through the glorious victory over the Spanish Armada. Queen Elizabeth was bitterly sad over his death. His son, Robert Cecil, became the new chief councilor, but he was no replacement for his father.

In the last years and months of her life, Queen Elizabeth sometimes regretted the things she had done. Perhaps she had been wrong in her decision to execute Mary, Queen of Scots. Perhaps she should have married at some point. Now, she had no one to talk to. William Cecil had been her closest advisor. Sir Walter Raleigh and the Earl of Essex had been her greatest friends. They were all gone now, either dead or in disgrace. Queen Elizabeth also saw trouble on the horizon. She had done very well against Spain and other outside foes, but she knew that there was trouble at home.

First, the House of Commons and the House of Lords became less helpful to her. In the past, the two houses, which made up Parliament, had been very helpful to the queen. They usually granted her the money she asked for, but times had changed. There was a new group in the House of Commons that wanted to limit the royal powers. Queen Elizabeth knew that she would get what she needed, but she worried about the future—about what her successor would do with the House of Commons and the House of Lords—and whom to name as her successor.

There was only one answer to that question. It had to be James VI, King of Scots. He was the only son of Mary, Queen of Scots. He had been a child when his mother fled to England and was imprisoned. He had never done anything to rescue his mother. In fact, he had been a strong ally of Queen Elizabeth's over the past 20 years. Given his blood relationship, and the fact that Queen Elizabeth had no children, King James had to be her successor.

Queen Elizabeth was worried about something else, too—religion. During her reign, Elizabeth had

As Queen Elizabeth neared the end of her life, she decided that James VI, King of Scots—the only son of Mary, Queen of Scots—would be her successor upon her death. He became King James I of England.

been a strong Protestant, but she had not tried to force England's Catholics to convert to her faith. This had made some of the hard-line Protestants angry. They formed a group called the Puritans. They wanted to purify the church.

Queen Elizabeth did not like the Puritans and she made life difficult for them. As she headed into her later years, Queen Elizabeth was worried that the Puritans would make trouble. She could not have known that some of them would cross the Atlantic Ocean to start new colonies, but one group of them—the Pilgrims—would indeed come to Plymouth, Massachusetts, to start a new life.

In November 1603, Queen Elizabeth met her Parliament for the last time. She gave what is known as her golden speech. She told the members of the House of Commons and the House of Lords that she loved them. She told them that, even though there might be greater kings or queens in the future, none would love them as much as she had. As she left Parliament, the members bowed their heads. They knew she was the greatest ruler of their time.

Soon after her famous speech, Queen Elizabeth's health began to decline. She was tired more often.

She even stumbled sometimes. For a woman who had danced throughout her life, this was a difficult transition. She grew even weaker in the winter of 1603.

One day, toward the end of her life, Queen Elizabeth sat on a pile of cushions in the middle of a room. She was too tired to move. Robert Cecil, the son of William Cecil, came forward. He said, "Your Majesty, for the sake of the people, you must go to bed." Queen Elizabeth turned slowly. "*Must, must.* Little man, little man, you do not use that word with princes. Were your father still alive, you would not dare say it."[20] Queen Elizabeth got up, but a little while later she went to bed and never really got out of it again. She died on March 24, 1603, a few months before her seventieth birthday.

Queen Elizabeth's funeral was the grandest event seen in many years. Horses draped in black pulled the funeral chariot. The queen lay in her coffin, on top of which there was a wooden image of her. People wept openly. Queen Elizabeth was dead, and England's Golden Age had died with her. Even though there were years of prosperity and victory in the future, nothing would ever mean as much to the

Queen Elizabeth's Tomb

When Queen Elizabeth died, the citizens of England grieved the loss of their queen. A magnificent funeral took place. Elizabeth's body was brought to Westminster Abbey, where many of England's great leaders, warriors, authors, and statesmen are buried. Today, visitors who enter Westminster Abbey will find more than 2,000 monuments. Entering on the right, there are aisles of statues of great figures, such as Horatio Nelson and Major John Andre (a British martyr from the American Revolution). Almost at the end of the aisle, on the right side, is Poet's Corner, where many great men and women poets are buried.

The Coronation Chair and the Stone of Scone, symbols of British and Scottish royalty, can be found in the back. Continuing to the left is the Lady Chapel, where Queen Elizabeth and her half sister Queen Mary are buried next to each other. Queen Elizabeth's marble tomb is bright with color, as if to show off the colorful queen, who so impressed her people.

On the left side, passing along the aisles, are the tombs of many great figures from English history. A walk through Westminster Abbey provides one of the best ways to experience the grandeur and ceremony of England's past.

Queen Elizabeth I died on March 24, 1603, a few months before her seventieth birthday. Her funeral (shown here) was a grand event in England.

English people as Queen Elizabeth. She was their glorious queen and she would be missed.

Queen Elizabeth made history. She was one of those rare people who came forward at an important time to do great things. Though some 400 years have passed since her death, we still remember Queen Elizabeth, and her legacy, which will live on for many years to come.

Test Your Knowledge

1 By the end of 1599, Queen Elizabeth had been in power for how many years?

    a. 33

    b. 42

    c. 45

    d. 54

2 James VI, King of Scots was

    a. the cousin of Mary, Queen of Scots.

    b. the ex-husband of Mary, Queen of Scots.

    c. the brother of Mary, Queen of Scots.

    d. the only son of Mary, Queen of Scots.

3 The religious group that wanted to purify the church was known as

    a. the Puritans.

    b. the Innocents.

    c. the Naturals.

    d. the Authentics.

4 In what year did Queen Elizabeth meet her Parliament for the last time?

    a. 1630

    b. 1656

    c. 1603

    d. 1660

5 Queen Elizabeth died a few months before which birthday?

    a. Her seventieth

    b. Her fiftieth

    c. Her sixtieth

    d. Her fortieth

ANSWERS: 1. b; 2. d; 3. a; 4. c; 5. a

1533 Elizabeth is born to Henry VIII and Anne Boleyn.

1534 Henry VIII creates the new English Catholic Church.

1536 Anne Boleyn is beheaded for treason and adultery.

1537 Henry VIII and Jane Seymour have a son, Prince Edward.

1543 Mary, Queen of Scots is born.

1547 Henry VIII dies and is succeeded by Edward VI.

1549 Edward VI and his ministers approve the new *Book of Common Prayer,* making England a Protestant nation.

1553 Edward VI dies and is succeeded by Queen Mary I.

1533 Elizabeth is born to Henry VIII and Anne Boleyn

1543 Mary, Queen of Scots is born

1530

1537 Henry VIII and Jane Seymour have a son, Prince Edward

1547 Henry VIII dies and is succeeded by Edward VI

1554   Queen Elizabeth spends some time in the Tower of London.

1557   Many English Protestants die at the stake for refusing to renounce their religion.

1558   Queen Mary I dies and is succeeded by Queen Elizabeth I.

1560   Robert Dudley's wife dies.

1568   Mary, Queen of Scots comes to England.

1580   Francis Drake comes home after sailing around the world.

1581   Queen Elizabeth knights Francis Drake.

1558 Queen Mary I dies and is succeeded by Queen Elizabeth I

1588 English forces defeat the Spanish Armada

1610

1553 Edward VI dies and is succeeded by Queen Mary I

1587 Queen Elizabeth orders that Mary, Queen of Scots be executed

1603 Queen Elizabeth dies

1587 Queen Elizabeth orders that Mary, Queen of Scots be executed.

1588 English forces defeat the Spanish Armada.

1588 Robert Dudley dies.

1590 The colonists at the Roanoke colony mysteriously disappear.

1598 King Philip of Spain dies.

1601 The Earl of Essex is executed.

1603 Queen Elizabeth dies.

NOTES

CHAPTER 2:
We Wished for Our Elizabeth

1. Leah S. Marcus et al., eds.,
   Elizabeth I, Collected Works.
   Chicago: University of Chicago
   Press, 2000, p. 14.
2. Ibid., pp. 14–15.
3. Ibid., p. 15.
4. Ibid.
5. Ibid., p. 41.
6. Ibid.
7. Ibid.
8. Ibid., p. 42.
9. Jasper Ridley, *Elizabeth I: The
   Shrewdness of Virtue.* New York:
   Viking, 1988, p. 68.
10. Carolly Erickson, *The First
    Elizabeth.* New York: Summit
    Books, 1983, p. 163.

CHAPTER 3:
The Queen and Her Suitors

11. Robin Maxwell, *The Queen's
    Bastard.* New York: Arcade
    Publishing, Available online at
    http://www.arcadepub.com/
    Book/index.cfm?GCOI=55970
    100658400&fa=preview
12. Marcus et al., *Elizabeth I,
    Collected Works,* p. 71.

CHAPTER 4:
First Cousins, Once Removed

13. Marcus et al., *Elizabeth I,
    Collected Works,* p. 66.
14. Ibid., p. 130.
15. Ibid.
16. Ibid.

CHAPTER 7
The Preemptive Strike

17. Marcus et al, *Elizabeth I,
    Collected Works,* p. 131.

CHAPTER 8:
The Spanish Armada

18. Peter Padfield, *Maritime
    Supremacy and the Opening of
    the Western Mind.* New York:
    Overlook Press, 1999,
    p. 35.
19. Ridley, *Elizabeth I: The
    Shrewdness of Virtue,*
    p. 286.

CHAPTER 10:
End of the Golden Age

20. Mary M. Luke, *Gloriana:
    The Years of Elizabeth I.*
    New York: Coward, McCann
    & Geoghegan, 1973,
    p. XX.

Erickson, Carolly. *The First Elizabeth.* New York: Summit Books, 1983.

Luke, Mary M. *Gloriana: The Years of Elizabeth I.* New York: Coward, McCann & Geoghegan, 1973.

Marcus, Leah S. et al., eds. *Elizabeth I: Collected Works.* Chicago: University of Chicago Press, 2000.

Maxwell, Robin. *The Queen's Bastard.* New York: Arcade Publishing, Available online at http://www.arcadepub.com/Book/index.cfm ?GCOI=55970100658400&fa=preview

Padfield, Peter. *Maritime Supremacy and the Opening of the Western Mind.* New York: Overlook Press, 1999.

Ridley, Jasper. *Elizabeth I: The Shrewdness of Virtue.* New York: Viking, 1988.

Sugden, John. *Sir Francis Drake.* New York: Henry Holt & Company, 1990.

Books

Brimacombe, Peter. *All the Queen's Men: The World of Elizabeth I.* New York: Palgrave Macmillan, 2000.

Doran, Susan. *Queen Elizabeth I.* New York: New York University Press, 2003.

Hibbert, Christopher. *The Virgin Queen: Elizabeth I, Genius of the Golden Age.* Boston: Addison Wesley Publishing Company, 1992.

Stanley, Diane and Peter Vennema. *Good Queen Bess: The Story of Elizabeth I of England.* New York: HarperCollins, 2001.

Thomas, Jane Resh. *Behind the Mask: The Life of Queen Elizabeth I.* New York: Clarion Books, 1998.

Weir, Alison. *The Life of Elizabeth I.* New York: Ballantine Books, 1999.

Websites

Elizabeth I
http://www.tudorhistory.org/elizabeth/

History of the Monarchy: Kings and Queens of England (to 1603)
http://www.royal.gov.uk/output/page46.asp

Modern History Sourcebook: Queen Elizabeth I Against the Spanish Armada, 1588
http://www.fordham.edu/halsall/mod/1588elizabeth.html

Modern History Sourcebook: Queen Elizabeth I of England (b. 1533, r. 1558–1603) Selected Writing and Speeches
http://www.fordham.edu/halsall/mod/elizabeth1.html

Queen Elizabeth I (1533–1603)
http://www.elizabethi.org/

Samuel Willard Crompton is a biographer and historian who lives in western Massachusetts. He is the author or editor of more than 30 books, many of them written for Chelsea House. He grew up watching television series like *Elizabeth I* and *The Six Wives of King Henry VIII* and has a special interest in sixteenth- and seventeenth-century England. Crompton is a major contributor to the American National Biography, published by Oxford University Press. He teaches history at Holyoke Community College.